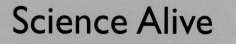

Science Alive

Electricity

Terry Jennings

FRANKLIN WATTS

LONDON•SYDNEY

An Appleseed Editions book

First published in 2008 by Franklin Watts

Franklin Watts
338 Euston Road, London NW1 3BH

Franklin Watts Australia
Level 17/207 Kent St, Sydney, NSW 2000

© 2008 Appleseed Editions

Appleseed Editions Ltd
Well House, Friars Hill, Guestling, East Sussex TN35 4ET

Created by Q2A Media
Series Editor: Honor Head
Book Editor: Harriet McGregor
Senior Art Designers: Ashita Murgai, Nishant Mudgal
Designer: Harleen Mehta
Picture Researcher: Poloumi Ghosh
Line Artists: Indernil Ganguly, Rishi Bhardhwaj
Illustrators: Kusum Kala, Sanyogita Lal

ISBN   978 0 7496 7560 8

Dewey classification: 537

All words in **bold** can be found in 'Words to remember' on pages 30–31.

Website information is correct at time of going to press. However, the publishers cannot
accept liability for any information or links found on third-party websites.

A CIP catalogue for this book is available from the British Library.

Picture credits
t=top b=bottom c=centre l=left r=right m=middle
Cover: Main Image: Bubbles Photolibrary / Alamy; Small Image: Wouter Tolenaars / Shutterstock
Atlantide Phototravel/ Corbis: 4, MvH/ istockphoto: 7, Milos Luzanin/ Shutterstock: 11,
H. Schmid/ zefa/ Corbis: 15, Juniors Bildarchiv/ Photolibrary: 18, Richard T Nowitz/ Photolibrary: 19,
paulaphoto/ Shutterstock: 20, Edward Hardam/ Shutterstock: 21, flashon/ Shutterstock: 25,
Vlad Valeyev/ Shutterstock: 26, Scholastic Studio 10/ Photolibrary: 28, Tihis/ Shutterstock: 29

Franklin V

Contents

What is electricity?

Electricity is a type of **energy**. Electricity gives power, light and heat to cities, towns and villages all over the world.

Sparks and currents

There are two types of electricity. You can see one type of electricity when you comb your hair and it stands on end. This is called **static electricity**. The other type of electricity flows through wires. This is called **current electricity**.

▲ *Current electricity makes these colourful signs light up.*

All change

Electricity can be changed into other types of energy. In a light bulb, electricity is changed into light. In an electric heater, electricity is changed into heat.

◀ *Electricity travels from a plug, through a wire and powers this lamp. Electrical energy has changed into light and heat energy.*

Static electricity

The first type of electricity that scientists discovered was static electricity. 'Static' means 'to stay still'. Static electricity usually stays in one place.

Rubbing

Static electricity is made when two materials rub together. Have you heard crackling sounds when you undress? That is static electricity. It is made when your clothes rub against you.

▼ *Static electricity attracts your hair to a comb. It usually happens when the weather is dry and bright. If the weather is damp, you may not see the effects of static electricity.*

Getting a shock

Lightning is also caused by static electricity. It builds up in storm clouds. When there is too much static electricity, it leaps to another cloud or to the ground. You see it as a flash of lightning.

▲ *Lightning is caused by static electricity. It is extremely powerful.*

Try this...

Jumping paper

You can find out more about static electricity by doing this simple experiment.

You will need
• tissue paper • scissors • a woolly jumper • a balloon

1 Ask an adult to help you cut or tear the paper into tiny pieces, the smaller the better.

2 Blow up the balloon. Rub it on the jumper.

3 Hold the balloon just above the pieces of paper.

What happened?

When you rubbed the balloon, static electricity collected on the balloon's surface. This means that the balloon became charged with static electricity. The paper was attracted to the charged balloon.

Currents

Electricity is most useful when it flows along a wire. This is called an electric current or current electricity. An electric current can power machines.

Circuits

A circuit is a path or loop that electricity can flow around. If you make a loop by connecting wires to a light bulb and to a **battery**, the bulb lights up. You have made an electric circuit. Electricity flows from the battery, through the bulb and back to the battery.

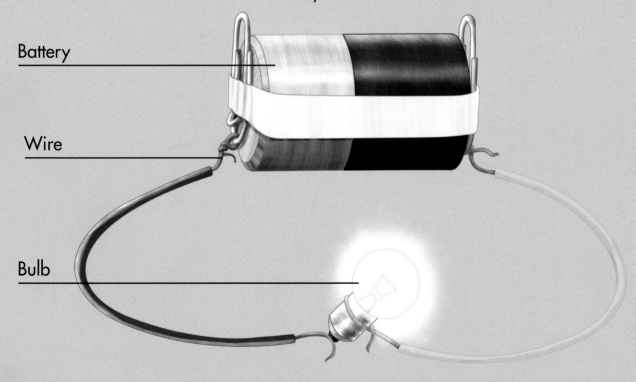

Battery

Wire

Bulb

▲ The battery produces an electric current. The battery pushes the electric current around the circuit.

Conductors and insulators

Materials that allow an electric current to flow through them are called **conductors**. Metals, such as copper and gold, are good conductors. **Insulators** are materials that an electric current cannot flow through easily. Plastic and rubber are good insulators.

▶ *An electric cable is made from a conductor and an insulator. The electric current flows through the metal conductor. The plastic insulator stops the electric current from escaping.*

Plastic insulator

Copper conductor

Try this...

Electric circuits

You can see how an electrical circuit works by building one.

You will need

• a wooden or plastic tray • a battery • two metal paperclips • sticky tape • two wires • a torch light bulb • a selection of objects – keys, coins, string, rubber bands, paper, paperclips

1 Set up the equipment on the tray as shown in the drawing.

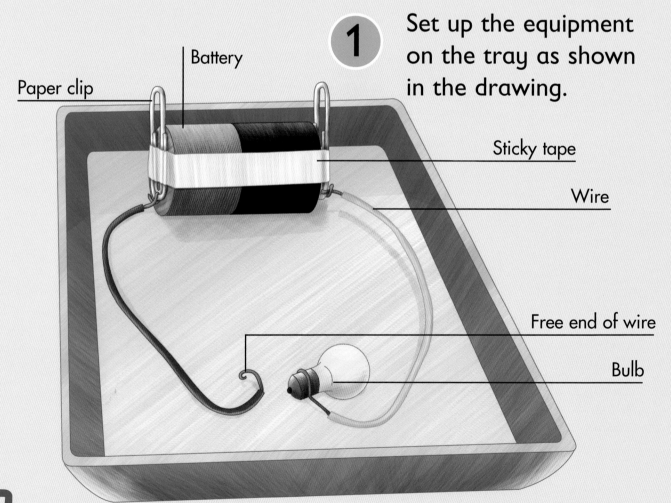

Paper clip

Battery

Sticky tape

Wire

Free end of wire

Bulb

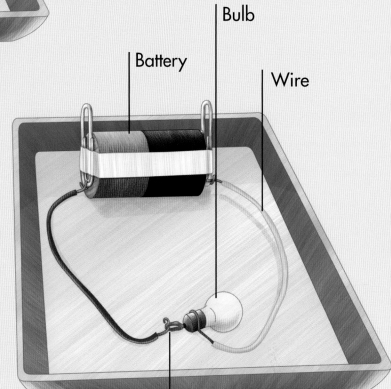

Touch the free end of the wire to the metal end of the bulb.

Bulb

Battery

Wire

Rubber band connecting the wire and bulb

3 Touch the free end of the wire against one end of one of your objects. Touch the other end of the object against the metal end of the bulb.

Repeat this with your other objects.

What happened?

When the wire touches the bulb, the circuit is complete. The battery pushes an electric current around the circuit. The bulb lights. When you connect some objects in the circuit, the bulb does not light. These objects are insulators. When you connect other objects in the circuit, the bulb lights. These objects are conductors.

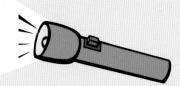

Using switches

We use electrical machines to do work for us at home. They heat water, wash clothes, clean dishes and suck dust off the floor. We turn them on and off with a **switch**.

On and off

When a switch is on, it completes the circuit and an electric current flows. When a switch is off, it makes a gap in the circuit. The electric current stops flowing.

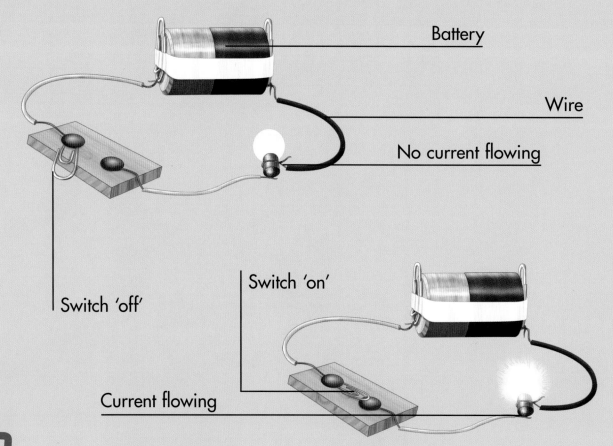

Battery

Wire

No current flowing

Switch 'off'

Switch 'on'

Current flowing

Mains electricity

The electric current that comes from a wall socket is called mains electricity. Mains electricity is very powerful. Never play around with it. It could burn you or even kill you.

◀ *Electricity from a mains socket needs to be powerful to work large machines, such as this washing machine.*

Try this...

Series and parallel

See what happens when you add extra bulbs to a circuit.

You will need

- a torch battery • six pieces of wire • sticky tape
- metal paper clips • three torch bulbs in bulb holders
- a small screwdriver

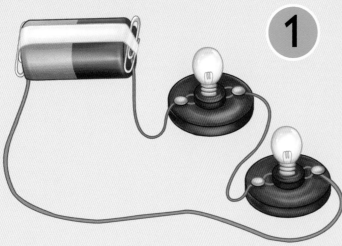

1 Make a circuit like the one in the picture. This is called a series circuit because the bulbs are in a series or row.

2 Now add an extra bulb to the circuit. Are the bulbs brighter or dimmer than before? Ask an adult to remove one of the bulbs. What happens to the other bulbs?

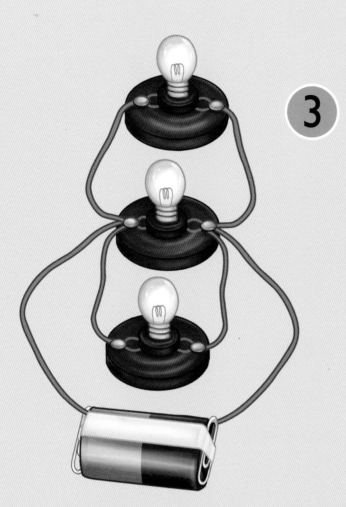

3 Now wire three bulbs like this. This is called a parallel circuit. Are the bulbs brighter or dimmer than before? Ask an adult to remove one of the bulbs. What happens to the other bulbs?

What happened?

In the series circuit, an extra bulb makes all the bulbs dimmer since they share the electrical current. When you remove one bulb, the other bulbs go out. In the parallel circuit, all the bulbs are equally bright. If one bulb is removed, the others stay alight.
Which type of circuit do you think you have in your home?

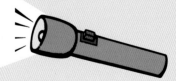

Electric animals

A few animals use electricity when they hunt for food. Some animals even use electricity to attack other creatures.

Electric fish

Electric currents flow through water. Some fish can sense electricity coming from their prey (animals they eat). They can even find animals hidden under sand.

▼ *The hammerhead shark uses its strangely shaped head to sense electric signals underwater.*

Zap!

The electric eel has muscles that can produce electricity. The eel can stun its prey with a powerful electric shock. If another animal attacks an electric eel… ZAP!

▲ *Some electric eels grow to more than one metre in length. Electric eels can store electricity like a battery.*

Batteries and bulbs

Batteries are containers filled with chemicals. They make electricity. All sorts of gadgets, such as watches, mobile phones and cameras, are powered by batteries.

▶ *Batteries let you use a laptop computer without having to plug it into the mains electricity supply.*

Chemicals

A battery turns chemicals into electrical energy. When you turn on a torch, electricity flows along a strip of metal from the battery to the bulb. The bulb glows. The battery makes electricity until its chemicals have been used up.

Bulbs

Electricity heats up the materials that it flows through. Inside some light bulbs is a very thin wire, called a filament. When electricity flows through the filament, it becomes so hot that it glows brightly.

Filament

▶ *You can see the thin filament in the centre of the light bulb. It eventually burns out and the light bulb must be replaced.*

Try this...
Making batteries

You can find out more about batteries by making one from a few simple materials.

You will need
• a lemon • a washed and clean paperclip • a washed and clean penny

 Squeeze and roll a lemon to make it juicier. Ask an adult to make two small slits in the lemon's skin.

2 Thoroughly wash the paperclip and the penny. Push the paperclip into one slit and push the penny into the other slit. They should not touch each other.

3 Put your tongue on the paperclip and the penny. Your tongue must touch both objects at the same time.

What happened?

When the metals touch the lemon juice, a chemical reaction begins. The reaction pushes an electric current from the paperclip to the penny. When you touch them with your tongue, you make a complete circuit. You may feel a tingle as the tiny current crosses your tongue. **Never try this with any other electricity source.**

23

Power stations

Most of the electricity we use in our homes, shops, factories and streets is mains electricity. It is made in large buildings called **power stations**.

Steam power

Most power stations burn a fuel, such as coal, oil or gas, to heat water. The water changes to steam. It rushes through pipes and hits paddle-wheels called **turbines**. The steam makes the turbines spin. The turbines drive huge electricity **generators**, which produce electricity.

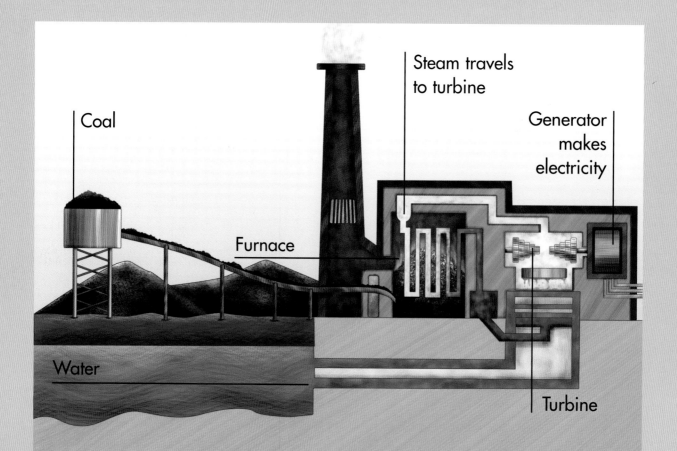

Coal

Steam travels to turbine

Generator makes electricity

Furnace

Water

Turbine

Cables

Electricity leaves the power station and travels along cables to wherever it is needed. Tall towers called pylons hold the cables above the ground. In cities, the cables may be below the ground.

◀ *It is important to stay away from pylons. They carry huge amounts of electricity and can be very dangerous.*

Green electricity

Making electricity by burning fuels produces gases. The gases collect in the air. They are making the Earth warmer. This is called **global warming**. Some ways of making electricity do not cause global warming.

Water power

The energy of moving water can be used to make electricity. A **dam** is built across a river so that a **reservoir** forms. Water from the reservoir passes through turbines. The turbines turn and spin generators. The generators produce electricity.

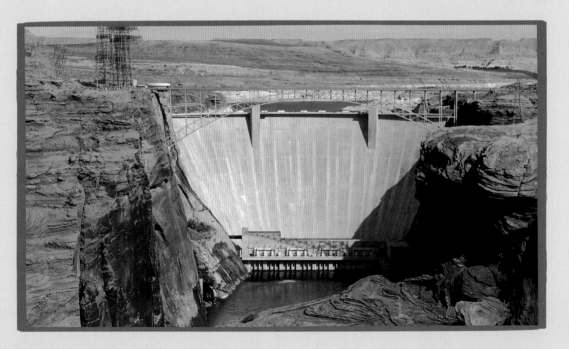

▲ *This dam makes electricity for homes, factories, shops and schools.*

Electricity from the wind

A **wind turbine** looks like a giant fan on top of a tall tower. The wind energy turns the blades and this drives a generator. The generator produces electricity.

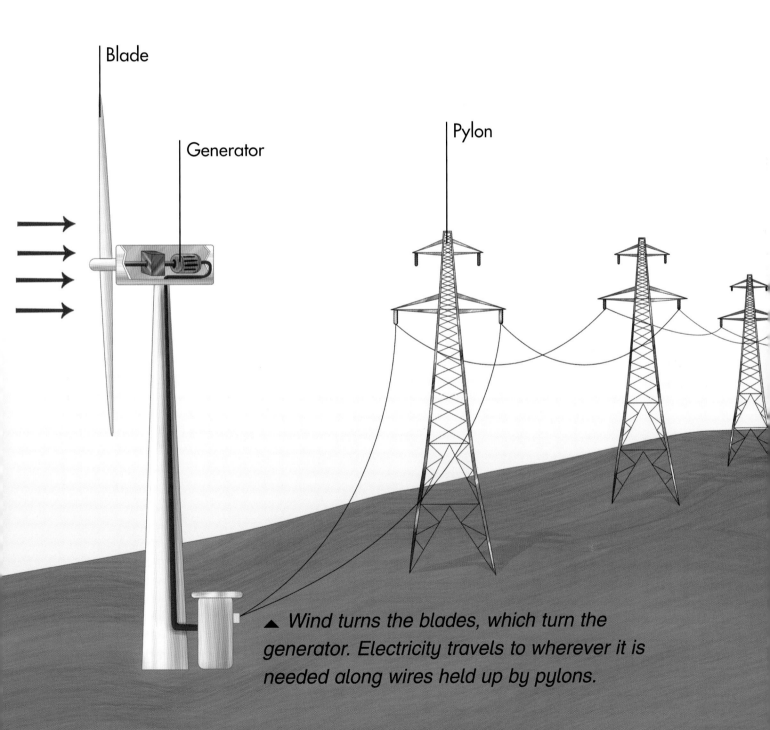

Blade

Generator

Pylon

▲ *Wind turns the blades, which turn the generator. Electricity travels to wherever it is needed along wires held up by pylons.*

Electronics

Sound, pictures and messages can all be changed into electricity. They can be sent a long way away very quickly.

Telephones

When you speak into a telephone, the sound is changed into electrical signals. These go down the wire to another telephone. The second telephone turns the electrical signals back into sounds.

◀ Mobile phones are electronic and need electricity to work. They send their signals through the air as radio waves.

Computers

A computer works using **microchips**. Microchips are tiny electrical circuits. They act as the computer's brain and its memory.

▲ *Each tiny rectangle here is a microchip. Each microchip contains thousands of electronic parts.*

Words to remember

Battery
A device that uses chemical energy to make electricity.

Conductor
A material that allows electricity to pass through it easily.

Current electricity
An electrical charge that moves through a wire.

Dam
A wall built across a river valley to hold back water.

Energy
Energy comes in many forms, including light, heat and electricity. It comes from fuels and other sources, such as wind and water.

Generator
A machine that changes movement energy into electricity.

Global warming
The warming of the Earth's atmosphere (air). Most scientists believe global warming is caused by gases produced when people burn coal, oil and gas.

Insulator

A material that does not allow electricity to pass through it.

Microchip

An electronic circuit containing lots of tiny parts.

Power station

A building where electricity is made and sent out for people to use.

Reservoir

A man-made lake often created by a dam.

Static electricity

Electricity that builds up on the surface of materials that do not conduct electricity.

Switch

A device that turns an electric current on and off.

Turbine

A paddle-wheel that spins when water, steam or air pushes against it. Turbines are often connected to generators.

Wind turbine

A machine that uses wind energy to produce electricity.

Index

Webfinder

www.aecl.ca/kidszone/atomicenergy/electricity/index.asp

www.bbc.co.uk/schools/ks2bitesize/science/revision_bites/conductors.shtml

www.sciencenewsforkids.org/

http://pbskids.org/zoom/activities/sci/

www.bbc.co.uk/schools/websites/4_11/site/science.shtml